Cooking Baking with I▌ Cream

Best Recipes for St Patrick's Day Beyond – Eat, Drink Be Merry!

BY

Christina Tosch

Copyright 2020 Christina Tosch

Copyright Notes

Table of Contents

Introduction

Give your go-to, after-dinner drink, Irish cream liqueur, a starring role in your kitchen and add some creamy goodness to your favorite recipes.

This luxury liqueur dates back nearly 50 years to the early seventies when Irish distilleries had an excess of alcohol and dairies a lot of extra milk. The two ingredients came together along with a handful of other flavorings to create the indulgent drink we know and love today, Irish cream liqueur.

Irish cream liqueur is a favorite yuletide and St Patrick's Day tipple. It not only rocks on the rocks though, as it can also be used in lots of creative culinary ways in your cooking and baking, too!

Cheesecake and cookies are just the beginning. Here, you will find recipes for not just desserts and sweet treats but savory dishes, drinks and more.

Eat, Drink Be Merry; Irish cream liqueur in your cooking and baking is a recipe for success!

Savory

Braised Short Ribs with Irish Creamed Cabbage

Enjoy a modern take on a classic Irish dish as Irish cream liqueur takes this hearty main to a whole new level.

Servings: 4

Total Time: 3hours 15mins

Ingredients:

- 3 pounds bone-in short ribs
- Kosher salt
- Freshly ground black pepper
- 2 tbsp vegetable oil
- 1 yellow onion (peeled and chopped)
- 4 cloves garlic (peeled and halved)
- 4 tbsp sherry vinegar
- 6 ounces Irish cream liqueur
- 3-4 cups chicken stock
- 8 cups warm water
- 2 tbsp salt
- 2 tbsp sugar
- 1 head green cabbage (cored and finely sliced)
- 2 tbsp butter

Directions:

1. Preheat the main oven to 300 degrees F.

2. Season the ribs liberally with kosher salt and black pepper.

3. Over moderate-low heat, heat a Dutch oven.

4. Add the oil to the Dutch oven and allow 5 minutes to preheat.

5. Using kitchen paper towel, pat the meat dry.

6. Add the ribs to the Dutch oven and brown on all sides.

7. Take the browned meat out of the Dutch oven.

8. Add the onions along with the garlic to the pan and sauté until fork tender for approximately 7-8 minutes.

9. Deglaze the pan with vinegar and reduce by 75 percent.

10. Next, add the Irish cream and bring it to boil.

11. Then, return the short ribs to the pan and pour in a sufficient amount of stock to cover by 50-70 percent.

12. Cover with a lid, then transfer to the main oven to cook for 2 hours.

13. While the meat cooks, fill a bowl with water. Add the salt along with the sugar, and whisk until entirely dissolved.

14. Next, add the sliced cabbage and set aside to marinate.

15. Once the meat is ready, remove from the pan and put it aside.

16. Using a sieve, strain the sauce. Remove and discard the onions along with the garlic.

17. Return the Dutch oven to the stove over moderate heat. Add the butter.

18. Drain the cabbage and fry the butter until it softens for 5-6 minutes.

19. Skim off and remove any surface fat from the sauce before pouring it into the pan containing the cabbage. Bring to boil and cook for an additional 3-4 minutes, until slightly thickened. Season to taste.

20. When you are ready to serve, pile the cabbage onto the plates.

21. Slice the ribs and arrange them on top of the cabbage.

22. Spoon the sauce over the top of the ribs and cabbage and enjoy.

Candied Bacon Cheeseburger with BBQ Sauce and Onion Rings

This burger is for adults only! Not only is the candied bacon glazed with Irish cream liqueur, but also the BBQ sauce is infused with whiskey, and the batter for the onion rings features Irish stout.

Servings: 4

Total Time: 1hour 30mins

Ingredients:

- Nonstick cooking spray

Candied Bacon:

- 8 slices thick-cut bacon
- ⅔ cup Irish cream liqueur
- ¼ cup brown sugar
- Pinch of black pepper
- Pinch of cayenne pepper

BBQ Sauce:

- ¼ cup ketchup
- ¼ cup whiskey
- 1 tbsp apple cider vinegar
- 1 tbsp Worcestershire sauce
- ½ tsp liquid smoke
- 1 tbsp brown sugar
- ¼ tsp chili powder

Patties:

- 1½ pounds ground beef chuck
- Pinch of salt
- Dash of pepper
- 4 slices Irish Cheddar cheese
- 4 hamburger buns (split)
- 4 slices of tomato

Onion Rings:

- Peanut oil (to fry)
- ¾ cup flour
- 1 sweet onion (cut into ¼"rings)
- ¼ cornstarch
- 1 tsp paprika
- ½ tsp baking powder
- ½ tsp garlic powder
- Pinch of salt
- Dash of black pepper
- 1 cup Irish stout

Directions:

1. First, preheat the main oven to 350 degrees F.

2. Next, spray a wire rack with nonstick cooking spray and place it on top of an aluminum foil-lined baking sheet.

3. For the candied bacon: Lay the slices of bacon out.

4. Over moderate-high heat, in a small size pan, combine the Irish cream with the brown sugar. Then, add a pinch each of black pepper and cayenne pepper. Bring to boil before the heat and simmer until thickened, for 10 minutes.

5. Brush the mixture over the slices of bacon, repeat this twice.

6. Transfer to the oven and cook for 10 minutes.

7. Remove the bacon from the oven and brush once again. Return to the oven, then cook for another 10minutes.

8. For the BBQ sauce: While the bacon is cooking, prepare the BBQ sauce.

9. Add all the ingredients (ketchup, whiskey, apple cider vinegar, Worcestershire sauce, liquid smoke, brown sugar, and chili powder) to a pan over moderate-high heat and bring to boil.

10. Gently boil for 25 minutes while frequently stirring until the mixture reduces by half.

11. For the patties: Evenly divide the beef into 4 portions. Season with salt and pepper.

12. Over moderate-high heat in a grill pan, arrange the burgers, seasoned side facing downwards.

13. Season the side facing upwards with salt and black pepper.

14. Grill the patties until charred, for 3-4 minutes on each side.

15. Transfer the grilled patties to the oven and bake until they register an internal temperature of 145 degrees F, this will take approximately 20 minutes.

16. Next, put a cheese slice on top of each patty and return to the oven for 60 seconds, until entirely melted. Take out of the oven and put to one side.

17. For the onion rings: Using kitchen paper towel line a baking sheet.

18. In a pan, heat the oil to a temperature of 350 degrees F.

19. In your bowl, combine the flour with the onion, cornstarch, paprika, baking powder, garlic powder, pinch of salt, dash of pepper and the Irish stout, and whisk until silky smooth.

20. When the oil reaches 350 degrees F, dip each onion ring into the batter. Carefully, and in batches, drop the battered onion rings into the oil.

21. Fry the onion rings until golden.

22. When you are ready to assemble: On the bottom half of your burger bun, place a slice of tomato followed by the cheeseburger. Add a dollop of BBQ sauce, 2 slices of candied bacon, and 2 onion rings.

23. Enjoy.

Filet Mignon with Irish Cream Sauce

Tender and juicy pan-fried steak is even better with a creamy, boozy sauce.

Servings: 2

Total Time: 20mins

Ingredients:

- 1 tbsp black pepper
- 1 tsp rosemary
- Pinch of salt
- Olive oil
- Knob of butter
- 2 beef tenderloin steaks (room temperature)

Sauce:

- ½ cup beef broth
- ½ tsp pepper
- 1 tbsp Irish cream liqueur
- 3½ ounces whipping cream
- ½ tsp mustard
- 1 tbsp Irish butter

Directions:

1. In a small bowl, combine the black pepper and rosemary.

2. Salt both sides of the steaks before pressing one side of each steak into the pepper seasoning to create a crust.

3. In a hot skillet, add a drop of oil and a knob of butter.

4. Sear the steaks to your preferred level of doneness.

5. Next, remove the steaks to a chopping board and set aside to rest for 5-10 minutes.

6. To prepare the sauce: Combine the beef broth with the pepper and cook until reduced by half.

7. Add the Irish cream liqueur, whipping cream, and mustard and reduce until you achieve your desired consistency.

8. Remove from the heat, then swirl in the Irish butter and allow to cool slightly and thicken.

9. Thinly slice the steaks and top with the Irish cream sauce.

Irish Cream and Whiskey Glazed Broiled Ham Steak

The glaze for this dish works equally as well for turkey and pork. Just make sure that you brush the glaze over during the final 5-10 minutes of cooking to avoid the sugar from burning.

Servings 4

Total Time: 12mins

Ingredients:

Glaze:

- ½ cup packed brown sugar
- ½ cup Irish whiskey
- ¼ cup Irish cream liqueur
- ¼ cup soy sauce
- ¼ cup ketchup
- 4 tbsp unsalted butter
- 2 tbsp heavy cream
- 2 tbsp freshly squeezed lemon juice
- ½ tsp fresh black pepper

Ham:

- 2-3 pounds ham steak (center cut and cooked)

Directions:

1. First, for the glaze: Combine all of the ingredients (brown sugar, Irish whiskey, Irish cream liqueur, soy sauce, ketchup, unsalted butter, heavy cream, lemon juice, and black pepper in a pan. Over moderate heat bring to simmer.

2. Simmer briskly for 5 minutes, until combined, thickened and flavorful.

3. For the ham: Preheat your grill. Then, using aluminum foil, line a shallow baking pan. Put a rack in the baking pan.

4. Place the ham steak on the rack.

5. Brush the glaze over the ham.

6. Broil the ham approximately 3-4"away for the heat source for 4 minutes, or until the glaze bubbles. Take care not to burn the sugar.

7. Turn the ham over and baste.

8. Broil for an additional 3-5 minutes.

9. Serve and enjoy.

Irish Cream Shrimp

Shrimp sautéed in garlic butter may taste good but add Irish cream liqueur to the mix, and you will have a great appetizer. Serve with lots of crusty bread to mop up the delicious sauce.

Servings: 8

Total Time: 10mins

Ingredients:

- Butter (as needed)
- 2 pounds jumbo shrimp (peeled and deveined)
- 2 garlic cloves (peeled and thinly sliced)
- A handful of fresh parsley (chopped)
- ¼ cup Irish cream liqueur
- Crusty bread (to serve, optional)

Directions:

1. In your hot frying pan, melt the butter.

2. Add the garlic to the butter and cook until browned. Add the parsley.

3. Pour in the Irish cream liqueur and stir for 2-3 minutes.

4. Add the shrimp to the pan and cook until they become pink. Flip them over and cook for an additional 1-2 minutes. Total cooking time will take approximately 4-6 minutes. The shrimp are fully cooked when they register an internal temperature of 165 degrees F.

5. Serve with crusty bread.

Mussels in White Wine and Irish Cream Sauce

France and Ireland come together to create the perfect seafood dish to serve with crisp, golden French fries. You will love to share this aromatic appetizer.

Servings: 2

Total Time: 30mins

Ingredients

- 1 (1pound) bag frozen French fries
- 2 tbsp Irish butter
- 2 tbsp onion (peeled and chopped)
- 2 tbsp leek (chopped)
- 2 pounds Irish mussels (washed and cleaned of debris)
- 3 tbsp French white wine
- 4 tbsp fish stock
- 2 tbsp runny honey
- 3tbsp Irish cream liqueur
- 4 tbsp cream
- Celtic seasoning salt
- Freshly squeezed juice of 1 lemon
- 4 scallions (chopped, to garnish)
- Bunch of parsley (to garnish)

Directions:

1. First, cook the French fries according to the package directions and keep warm.

2. Heat a pan with 2 tablespoons of butter. Add the onions and leek to the pan and sweat.

3. Next, add the mussels followed by the white wine, and fish stock, stirring to combine entirely.

4. Add the runny honey along with the Irish cream liqueur and cream. Bring to boil and continue to simmer until all the mussels are open. Remove and discard any unopened mussels.

5. Season with salt followed by a squeeze of fresh lemon juice.

6. Garish with chopped scallions and parsley and serve with a bowl of golden French fries.

St Patrick's Day Chicken with Mushrooms

On March 17 this year, why not serve up tender, pan-fried chicken paired with whiskey, Irish cream liqueur and juicy Portabello mushrooms?

Servings: 4

Total Time: 20mins

Ingredients:

- 2 boneless chicken breasts (halved)
- 2 tbsp clarified butter (divided)
- 4 Portobello mushrooms (sliced)
- 5-6 redskin potatoes (partially cooked and sliced or quartered)
- Salt and black pepper
- 1 cup flour
- 1 ounce Irish whiskey
- 2 ounces Irish cream liqueur

Directions:

1. Pound all 4 pieces of chicken breast.

2. In a sauté pan, heat 1½ tablespoons of butter. Add the mushrooms along with the potatoes to the pan. Season with salt and pepper.

3. Add the flour to a shallow bowl or dish.

4. Dredge the chicken in the flour.

5. Add the chicken to the pan along with the remaining butter and sauté for 3 minutes.

6. Add the Irish whiskey and carefully ignite. Once the whiskey burns off, add the Irish cream liqueur and simmer until combined.

7. Serve and enjoy.

Stuffed Chicken with Irish Cream Mushroom Sauce

Juicy chicken stuffed with bacon and served with a silky Irish cream and mushroom sauce is a restaurant-worthy main. Serve with green beans and potatoes.

Servings: 4

Total Time: 2hours 45mins

Ingredients:

- 4 (5 ounces) boneless, skinless chicken breast halves
- 1 cup bacon (coarsely chopped)
- 4 slices of Provolone cheese
- 3 tbsp water
- 8 red potatoes (cut into ¼ "thick slices)
- 1⅓ cups heavy cream (divided)
- 8 ounces mozzarella cheese (shredded)
- 4 slices of bacon
- 1½ pounds fresh green beans (trimmed)
- 7 ounces Irish cream liqueur (divided)
- ¼ cup heavy whipping cream
- ½ cup peanuts (chopped)
- 1 tbsp butter
- 6 ounces mushrooms (sliced)

Directions:

1. First, preheat the main oven to 375 degrees F.

2. With a sharp knife, slice a pocket into the thicker side of each chicken breast.

3. Spoon approximately 2 tablespoons of the chopped bacon into the middle of the Provolone cheese slice. Fold the cheese slice around the bacon and stuff it into the chicken breast's pocket.

4. Next, repeat the process with the remaining chicken breasts.

5. Then, place the stuffed breasts on a baking sheet and sprinkle with a drop of water.

6. Bake the chicken in the oven until the juices run clear, the bacon is sufficiently cooked, and the cheese is entirely melted. This will take approximately 60 minutes.

7. Add the potatoes to a pan and add sufficient water to cover, bring to boil.

8. Over moderate heat cook until the potatoes are fork-tender, for approximately 15 minutes. Drain thoroughly.

9. Over low heat, heat ⅔ cup of cream in a pan,

10. Stir in the shredded mozzarella and cook until melted.

11. Pour the cheese mixture into the pan with the potatoes and gently toss to coat evenly.

12. Add the bacon to a skillet over moderate heat and while occasionally turning cook for 5 minutes, until the bacon is soft and beginning to brown.

13. Drain the bacon fat and transfer the browned bacon to a plate and set aside to cool.

14. Wrap one slice of bacon around 10 green beans and with a toothpick, secure. Then, repeat the process with the remaining slices of bacon.

15. Add the bundles of beans to the skillet and over moderate heat, cook while frequently stirring until the bacon is crisp and the beans fork tender. This step will take approximately 10 minutes.

16. Add 2 ounces of Irish cream along with ⅔ cup of whipping cream into the skillet containing the green beans and cook over low heat. Spoon the mixture over the beans and garnish with chopped peanuts.

17. Over moderate heat, in a skillet, melt the butter. Cook the mushrooms while stirring until the majority of the liquid has evaporated, for approximately 10 minutes.

18. Stir the remaining 5 ounces of Irish cream along with the remaining 2/3 cup of whipping cream into the mushrooms over moderate heat. Bring the mixture to boil before reducing the heat to low and cooking for 10 minutes or until the sauce thickens.

19. To serve: Add the stuffed chicken to a plate, pour the mushroom sauce over the top and serve with green beans and potatoes.

20. Enjoy.

Sweet

After-Dinner Chocolates

These boozy after-dinner chocolate candies are sure to impress family and friends when you serve them at your next dinner party!

Servings: 30

Total Time: 1hour 15mins

Ingredients:

- 12 ounces semisweet chocolate chips
- ¼ cup heavy whipping cream
- ½ cup Irish cream liqueur
- 2 cups pecans (chopped)

Directions:

1. Cover a cookie sheet with wax paper.

2. Add the semisweet choc chips, heavy whipping cream, and Irish cream liqueur to a bowl and melt together using a microwave. This will take approximately 2½ minutes, remove every 30 seconds to stir.

3. Fold in the pecans.

4. Drop teaspoonfuls of the mixture onto the cookie sheets and chill for an hour until set before serving.

Banana and Irish Cream Fro-Yo

A lighter alternative to classic ice cream, this frozen yogurt is sweet and silky but also has that typical fro yo tang!

Servings: 6

Total Time: 40mins

Ingredients:

- 1 cup dark chocolate chips
- 1 cup Irish cream liqueur
- ½ cup honey
- ½ tsp sea salt
- 5 bananas
- 2 cups plain, low-fat Greek yogurt

Directions:

1. Add the choc chips to a processor and pulse until crumb-like.

2. Add the liqueur, honey, salt, bananas, and yogurt to the processor and blitz until smooth and combined with no chunks.

3. Transfer the batter to a resealable container and stir a few times using a spatula to remove any air bubbles.

4. Place in the freezer overnight to set before serving.

Boozy Chocolate Mousse

Served in individual cups, this rich and luscious mousse with silky Irish cream liqueur is the perfect St Patrick's Day sweet treat

Servings: 4

Total Time: 4hours 30mins

Ingredients:

- 6 tbsp Irish cream liqueur
- 4 ounces bittersweet chocolate
- 2 eggs (separated)
- 2 tbsp honey
- Whipped cream (to serve)

Directions:

1. Melt together the liqueur and chocolate in a saucepan over low heat, stir continually.

2. Whisk in the egg yolks and honey until glossy and combined. Take off the heat and allow to cool for 10 minutes.

3. In the meantime, whip up the egg whites until they can hold soft peaks. Fold the egg whites into the melted chocolate mixture until incorporated.

4. Divide the mixture evenly between 4 small serving cups. Cover each mug with plastic wrap and chill for 4 hours.

5. Top each portion with a dollop of whipped cream before serving.

Bread Pudding with Irish Cream Sauce

Boozy and buttery, this delicious bread pudding smothered in a sweet Irish cream sauce is as satisfying as it is tasty.

Servings: 8-10

Total Time: 10hours 15mins

Ingredients:

Pudding:

- ⅔ cup packed brown sugar
- 5 large size eggs
- 2⅔ cups skim milk
- ½ tsp ground cinnamon
- 2 tsp vanilla essence
- 9 cups (½") cubes of French bread (crusts removed)
- ¼ cup dates (pitted and chopped)
- ¼ cup golden raisins
- Nonstick cooking spray

Sauce:

- 2 tbsp brown sugar
- 2 egg yolks
- ½ cup skim milk
- 1 tbsp Irish cream liqueur

Directions:

1. For the pudding: In a bowl, combine the brown sugar with the eggs and using a whisk, stir to incorporate.

2. In a pan over moderate heat, heat the milk and cinnamon until small bubbles begin to form around the edges of the pan.

3. Gradually, while stirring continually with a whisk, add the hot milk mixture to the egg mixture.

4. Next, return the milk mixture to the pan and over low heat while continually stirring with a whisk cook until the mixture thickens to a custard.

5. Take the pan off the heat and stir in the vanilla essence.

6. In a bowl, combine the bread cubes with the dates and golden raisins.

7. Pour the milk mixture over the bread-raisin mixture and toss to well and evenly coat.

8. Spray an 8" baking dish with nonstick cooking spray.

9. Spoon the mixture into the dish, cover with a lid and place in the fridge overnight.

10. Preheat the main oven to 350 degrees F.

11. Put the baking dish inside a 13x9" baking ray. Pour in sufficient hot water to the pan to reach a 1" depth.

12. Cover and bake in the oven at 350 degrees for 20 minutes.

13. Remove the lid and bake for another 40 minutes, until springy to the touch.

14. For the sauce: In a bowl, and using a whisk, combine the brown sugar with the egg yolks.

15. Over moderate heat, in a pan, heat the milk, without boiling, until small bubbles form around the edges of the pan.

16. Gradually combine the hot milk with the egg yolk mixture while stirring continually using a whisk.

17. Add the milk mixture to a saucepan and over low heat, cook for 5-6 minutes, while stirring continuously until it easily coats the back of a wooden spoon.

18. Take off the heat and stir in the Irish cream liqueur.

19. Put the pan in a bowl filled with ice for 5 minutes while continually stirring until it has cooled to room temperature.

20. Serve the boozy sauce over the warm bread pudding and enjoy.

Cookie Dough Balls

A delicious, pop-in-the-mouth treat that makes the perfect food edible gift for over-21 members of the family and friends!

Servings: 20

Total Time: 30mins

Ingredients:

- 1 cup confectioner's sugar
- 3 cups vanilla wafer cookies (crushed)
- ⅓ cup Irish cream liqueur
- ⅓ cup corn syrup
- 12 ounces chocolate chips

Directions:

1. Cover a cookie sheet with parchment paper and set to one side.

2. Combine the confectioner's sugar and crushed cookies in a bowl.

3. Stir in the liqueur and corn syrup until the mixture is crumbly.

4. Taking 1 tbsp of the cookie dough at a time, roll into balls.

5. Melt the chocolate chips using a microwave, stir until silky.

6. Dip each dough ball in the chocolate mixture to coat evenly then transfer to the prepared cookie sheet. Then, let sit at room temperature until the chocolate sets.

7. Keep chilled until ready to serve.

Creamy Custard

Enjoy this silky custard on its own, pour it over pudding or pie or spoon it with ice cream. However, you decide to serve it, one thing is sure, it's a real winner.

Servings: 6-8

Total Time: 15mins

Ingredients:

- 2 cups whole milk
- ½ cup Irish cream liqueur
- 4 egg yolks
- 1 tsp vanilla essence
- ½ cup caster sugar
- 2 tbsp cornflour

Directions:

1. In a pan, combine the milk with the Irish cream and over moderate heat, stir to incorporate, bringing the mixture nearly to boiling point.

2. Take the pan off the heat and put aside to slightly cool.

3. In a large bowl, whisk the egg yolks with the cornflour, sugar, and vanilla essence, until thickened.

4. A little at a time, whisk then in the warm milk mixture.

5. Return the mixture to the pan and over moderate heat while stirring heat until the mixture thickens and boils, for 4-5 minutes.

6. Transfer to a mixing bowl and put to one side, while frequently stirring.

7. To prevent a skin forming, cover the surface of the bowl with kitchen wrap, and transfer to the fridge to chill.

8. Serve and enjoy.

Creamy Rice Pudding with Currants

Give a childhood favorite dessert an adult twist and top it with Irish cream liqueur.

Servings: 6

Total Time: 1hour 15mins

Ingredients:

- ¾ cup dried currants
- Butter (to grease, as needed)
- 4 cups whole milk (divided)
- 1 cup arborio rice
- ⅔ cup sugar
- ½ cup Irish cream liqueur
- Butter cookies (to serve)

Directions:

1. To plump the currants: Add the currants to a bowl and cover with boiling water. Then, allow to steep for 10-15 minutes before straining.

2. Preheat the main oven to 300 degrees F.

3. Lightly grease a 9" square baking dish with butter.

4. In a pan, bring 3 cups of milk to simmer.

5. Add the rice along with the sugar and stir until the sugar entirely dissolves.

6. Next, evenly spread the mixture in the prepared baking dish and loosely cover with aluminum foil. Bake in the preheated oven for half an hour.

7. Stir and continue to bake until the rice is bite tender for an additional 30 minutes.

8. Remove from the oven and stir in the remaining milk along with the soaked currants. Allow to cool.

9. Evenly divide the rice pudding amount 6 glasses. Top with Irish cream liqueur and serve with the butter cookies.

Dark Chocolate and Irish Cream Macarons

Dark chocolate macarons are spiked with a generous glug of Irish cream liqueur for an adult treat, guaranteed not to last long!

Servings: 30

Total Time: 8hours 40mins

Ingredients:

- ⅔ cup granulated sugar
- Whites of 2 large eggs
- 1¾ ounces ground almonds
- 1 tbsp cocoa powder
- 5¼ ounces dark chocolate ganache
- ¼ cup butter (chopped)
- ½ cup Irish cream liqueur

Directions:

1. Preheat the man oven to 355 degrees F.

2. Using an electric whisk, whip up the sugar and egg whites until the mixture can hold stiff peaks and is glossy.

3. Fold in the ground almonds and cocoa powder. Transfer the mixture to a piping bag.

4. Pipe the macaron batter onto a baking sheet in 60 equally-sized discs. Then, wet your finger and smooth out any peaks created by the piping bag.

5. Place in the oven and bake for 15 minutes. Turn the oven off and crack open the door, but do not take the macarons out of the oven for 5 minutes. After the 5 minutes, take the macarons out of the oven and allow to cool completely.

6. Add the ganache and butter to a bowl.

7. Pour the liqueur into a saucepan and bring to a simmer. Pour the liqueur over the ganache and butter and stir together until melted and smooth. Spoon the mixture into a piping bag with a star tip.

8. Pipe the mixture onto half of the cooled macarons, sandwich together with the remaining macarons to create 30 macarons. Allow to cool completely before serving.

Fancy French Toast

Whether you serve this boozy French toast for brunch or lunch, as a lite bite or supper snack, one thing is for sure you won't be able to stop at just one slice.

Servings: 4

Total Time: 15mins

Ingredients:

- Butter (to fry)
- 3 large size eggs
- ½ cup Irish cream liqueur
- 1 tsp vanilla essence
- 8 (1") slices brioche
- Confectioner's sugar (to dust)
- Syrup (to serve)
- Whipped cream (to serve)
- Sprinkles (to garnish)

Directions:

1. In a large size frying pan, over moderate heat, melt the butter.

2. In a bowl, whisk the eggs with the Irish cream and vanilla essence.

3. Dip each side of the slices of bread in the egg-vanilla mixture and add them to the pan. You may need to add more butter to the pan as necessary.

4. Serve with syrup, whipped cream, and garnish with sprinkles.

Frozen Irish Cream Granita

This adult slush puppy is refreshing either on its own or paired with fresh berries and a drizzle of Irish cream liqueur.

Servings:

Total Time: 3hours 20mins

Ingredients:

- 5¼ ounces granulated sugar
- 1½ pints water
- ½ cup Irish cream liqueur
- 1⅓ cups granulated sugar
- 3 cups water
- ⅔ cup Irish cream liqueur

Directions:

1. Over low heat, in a pan, dissolve the sugar in the water.

2. Take the pan off the heat and set aside to completely cool.

3. When the syrup is entirely cold, stir in the Irish cream.

4. Pour the mixture into a shallow freezer-safe bowl and freeze until its edges are frozen. Stir vigorously before returning to the freezer.

5. Repeat the process 6-8 times at approximately 30-60 minute intervals until the granite is frozen. This will take approximately 3 hours.

6. When you are ready to serve using a fork, scuff up the granita.

7. Use the granita within 1 day of making.

Fudge Swirl Irish Cream Ice Cream

Boozy ice cream for adults is the latest trend, and this frozen dessert recipe with Irish cream liqueur is a real keeper.

Servings: 8

Total Time: 8hours 12mins

Ingredients:

Fudge Swirl:

- ¾ cup semi-sweet chocolate chips
- ¼ cup heavy cream
- 2 tbsp Irish whiskey

Ice cream:

- 2 cups heavy cream
- 1 (14 ounces) can sweetened condensed milk
- ¼ cup Irish cream liqueur

Directions:

1. For the fudge swirl: Add the chocolate chips to a bowl and in the microwave, melt for 10-15 seconds, stirring every 3-5 seconds. Stir well until the chocolate is entirely melted and silky smooth.

2. Pour the heavy cream over the melted chocolate, stir to combine, and allow to rest for a few minutes.

3. Add the Irish whiskey and stir to incorporate. Set to one side to cool while you prepare the base.

4. For the ice cream base: In a large-size bowl, beat the cream to form stiff peaks.

5. Pour in the condensed milk followed by the Irish cream liqueur and stir until smooth and combined.

6. Transfer the ice cream base into an 8" square baking dish and spread out into an even layer.

7. In a parallel line, drizzle the fudge swirl over the ice cream and with a blunt knife swirl not stir into the ice cream.

8. Using kitchen wrap, cover the dish and place in the freezer overnight to set.

Fully-Loaded Chocolate Bark

This delicious chocolate bark is loaded with cranberries, sultanas, cookies, nuts, and, most importantly Irish cream liqueur! A flavor and texture sensation.

Servings: 6-8

Total Time: 30mins

Ingredients:

- 14 ounces milk chocolate (broken into pieces)
- 7 ounces white chocolate (broken into pieces)
- 3 tbsp Irish cream liqueur
- ½ cup sultanas
- ½ cup dried cranberries
- 1 cup honey-roasted nuts
- 6 butter cookies (crushed)

Directions:

1. Cover a cookie sheet with parchment paper. Then, set to one side.

2. Using a microwave separately melt the milk and white chocolate.

3. Allow the milk chocolate to completely cool and then stir in the Irish cream liqueur.

4. Next, Pour the milk chocolate onto the parchment paper and spread out into an even layer.

5. Scatter over the sultanas, cranberries, nuts, and cookies.

6. Drizzle over the white chocolate. Use your knife or skewer to swirl the white chocolate into the milk chocolate.

7. Chill for an hour or until set before breaking into shards and enjoying.

Irish Coffee Crème Brulee

No Irish cream recipe book would be complete without an indulgent Crème Brulee. What's more, don't wait for St Patrick's Day to come around to discover this decadent dessert.

Servings: 4

Total Time: 1hour 10mins

Ingredients:

- 4 medium-size egg yolks
- Pinch of sea salt
- 3 tbsp white sugar
- ⅔ cup heavy cream
- Scrapings of 1 vanilla bean
- 2 tbsp Irish cream liqueur
- ¼ cup freshly brewed espresso (cooled)
- Water (hot, as needed)
- 4 tbsp granulated sugar

Directions:

1. Preheat the main oven to 300 degrees F.

2. Place 4 small size ramekins inside a baking dish. Put aside.

3. In a mixing bowl, whisk the egg yolks along with the sea salt and white sugar.

4. Over medium heat, in a pan, cook the heavy cream until it begins to shimmer.

5. A little at a time, whisk then the hot cream into the egg yolk mixture until incorporated.

6. Next, whisk in the scrapings from the vanilla bean followed by the Irish cream and cool coffee.

7. Pour the mixture equally into the 4 ramekins.

8. Add sufficient hot water to the baking dish to reach halfway up the ramekins.

9. Next, bake in the preheated oven for 40 minutes.

10. Scatter 1 tablespoon of sugar on top of each ramekin and with a kitchen torch, caramelize the sugar.

11. Serve and enjoy.

Irish Cream Cheesecake

If you are planning a special occasion, get baking, and enjoy this heavenly cheesecake with its tangy Irish cream topping and salty-sweet cookie base.

Servings: 10

Total Time: 8hours 40mins

Ingredients:

- Butter (to grease)

Crust:

- 26 oreo cookies
- Pinch salt
- 4 tbsp melted butter

Topping:

- 1½ cups granulated sugar
- 2 pounds cream cheese (at room temperature)
- ¼ cup cornstarch
- 4 eggs
- ⅔ cup Irish cream liqueur
- 1 tsp vanilla essence

Directions:

1. Preheat 325 degrees F. Grease an 8" springform tin and arrange on a baking sheet.

2. First, prepare the crust. Add the cookies, salt, and melted butter to a food processor and blitz until wet and sandy.

3. Press the mixture into the base of the springform tin. Set to one side.

4. Next, make the topping. Beat together the sugar and cream cheese until fluffy. Whisk in the cornstarch and then the eggs, one at a time.

5. Finally, fold in the liqueur and vanilla essence.

6. Spoon the topping mixture over the crust in the springform tin.

7. Place in the oven and bake for just under 1½ hours until the cheesecake is mostly set. It should be only a little wobbly in the very center.

8. Take out of the oven and allow to cool completely before chilling overnight.

9. Slice and serve.

Irish Cream Wedge Scones

Take a quintessentially English afternoon tea nibble and give it an Emerald Isle makeover with indulgent Irish cream liqueur. You won't regret it!

Servings: 8

Total Time: 45mins

Ingredients:

Scones:

- ½ cup sour cream
- ½ tsp vanilla essence
- 1 egg
- ¼ cup Irish cream liqueur
- 2¼ cups all-purpose flour
- 1 tbsp baking powder
- 2 tbsp sugar
- ½ tsp salt
- 8 tbsp unsalted butter (cut into cubes)
- ½ cup caramel-flavored baking chips
- 1½ tbsp heavy cream
- Coarse sprinkling sugar

Glaze:

- ½ cup confectioner's sugar
- 2 tbsp Irish cream liqueur
- ½ tsp vanilla essence

Directions:

1. For the scones: Preheat the main oven to 400 degrees. Using parchment paper, line a baking sheet.

2. In your bowl, whisk the sour cream with the vanilla essence, egg, and Irish cream liqueur. Put to one side.

3. To a food processor, add the flour, baking powder, sugar, salt, and butter. On the pulse setting, process to a fine sand-like consistency.

4. In a large bowl, stir the flour mixture along with the wet ingredients and caramel baking chips until just combined. At this stage, your dough will be slightly crumbly.

5. Next, turn the dough out onto the prepared baking sheet and form into an 8" round.

6. Using heavy cream, brush the surface of the scone dough and scatter with coarse sugar.

7. Take a sharp kitchen knife and cut the dough into 8 wedges.

8. Pull the wedges slightly apart from each other and bake in the oven for 20-25 minutes, until baked through and golden brown.

9. Remove from the pan, then allow to completely cool on a baking rack.

10. For the glaze: In a bowl, whisk the confectioner's sugar with the Irish cream liqueur and vanilla essence until silky smooth.

11. Lastly, drizzle the glaze over the cooled scones and serve.

Millionaire's Shortbread

A British favorite, shortbread cookies have a buttery, melt-in-the-mouth texture. These particular cookies are topped with layers of boozy caramel and sweet chocolate and are ideal for enjoying alongside your afternoon tea and coffee.

Servings: 16

Total Time: 30mins

Ingredients:

Shortbread:

- ¾ cup sugar
- ¾ cup butter (at room temperature)
- 2 cups all-purpose flour
- Toffee:
- ½ cup butter
- 1 (14 ounces) can sweetened condensed milk
- ½ cup brown sugar
- 2 tbsp light corn syrup
- 2 tbsp Irish cream liqueur

Chocolate:

- 8 ounces semisweet choc chips
- 3 tbsp butter

Directions:

1. First, preheat the main oven to 350 degrees F.

2. First, make the shortbread dough. Then, beat together the sugar and butter until creamy. Add the flour and mix until well combined.

3. Press the dough into a 9" square baking tin.

4. Place in the oven and bake for just under half an hour until golden brown. Take out of your oven and allow to cool.

5. Next, make the toffee. In a saucepan over moderate heat, melt the butter. Add the condensed milk, brown sugar, and corn syrup. Stir continually and bring to a boil for 5 minutes.

6. Take off the heat and stir in the Irish cream.

7. Pour the toffee over the cool shortbread in the baking tin. Allow to cool completely.

8. Finally, prepare the chocolate layer. Melt together the choc chips and butter in a saucepan over moderately low heat. Stir until silky.

9. Pour the melted chocolate over the toffee layer and smooth out evenly using the back of a smooth. Chill until set before slicing into 16 squares.

Mini Mince Pies with Irish Cream

Why wait for Christmas to whip up a batch of these mini mince pies. Instead, celebrate the Emerald Isle all-year-round and, instead of serving with cream, enjoy with a generous glug of Irish cream liqueur.

Servings: 24

Total Time: 40mins

Ingredients:

- 13 ounces all-butter shortcrust pastry
- 1 egg (beaten)
- Sugar (to sprinkle)
- Powdered sugar (to serve)
- Irish cream liqueur (to serve)

Filling:

- 7 ounces mincemeat
- Zest of 1 tangerine or clementine
- 2 tbsp pecans (chopped)

Directions:

5. Preheat the main oven to 93 degrees F.

6. Cut off ⅓ of the shortcrust pastry and put it to one side.

7. Roll the remaining pastry out onto a clean, floured work surface to the thickness of a coin. Using a 2⅓" pastry cutter, cut out 12 pastry circles.

8. Lay the circles in a 24-cup mini muffin pan and transfer to the freezer while you roll out the other smaller ⅓ piece of pastry.

9. With a 1" star shape pastry cutter, create 24 stars. Place the stars on a plate and place in the freezer while you prepare the filling.

10. To prepare the filling: In a bowl, combine the mincemeat with the tangerine zest and pecans.

11. Spoon equal amounts of the filling into each muffin cup in the now chilled muffin tin.

12. Top with a pastry star and lightly brush with beaten egg.

13. Scatter with sugar and bake in the oven until golden for 20-25 minutes.

14. Remove from the oven and allow to slightly cool while still in the pan.

15. Take the pies out of the pan and dust with powdered sugar.

16. Pour Irish cream liqueur over the top and serve.

Mint Chip Irish Cream Fudge

Fudge is a classic treat for a reason! Its creamy, chewy texture and sweet milky flavor make this sweet candy addictive - beware though, one square is never enough!

Servings: 64

Total Time: 5hours 30mins

Ingredients:

- 1 cup unsweetened condensed milk
- 3½ cups milk chocolate chips
- 1 tsp vanilla essence
- ¼ cup Irish cream liqueur
- ½ cup mint baking chips

Directions:

1. Line an 8" square baking tin with aluminum foil.

2. Next, melt together the condensed milk and chocolate chips using a microwave, stir until silky.

3. Stir in the vanilla essence and Irish cream liqueur.

4. Pour the mixture into the prepared baking tin and sprinkle over the mint baking chips.

5. Cover with plastic wrap and chill for 4-5 hours until firm before slicing into squares.

Over-21 Marshmallows

Take this candy treat to the next level and infuse fluffy marshmallows with Irish cream. Enjoy on their own as a sweet snack or float them on top of hot chocolate.

Servings: N/A*

Total Time: 8hours 25mins

Ingredients:

- 3 (¼ ounce) sachets flavor-free gelatin
- ½ cup ice cold water
- ½ cup Irish cream
- 1½ cups white sugar
- 1 cup light corn syrup
- Nonstick cooking spray
- 1 cup confectioner's sugar

Directions:

1. Add the gelatin to the cold water in a stand mixer bowl fitted with a whisk.

2. In a pan, combine the Irish cream with the white sugar, and light corn syrup. Place the pan over moderate-high heat, cover with a lid, and cook for 3 minutes.

3. Remove the lid and continue cooking until the mixture registers 240 degrees F, this will take 7-8 minutes. Once this temperature is reached, remove your pan from the heat source.

4. At low speed, and while the mixer is running, gradually pour the sugar syrup down the sides of the mixer bowl into the gelatin. When all the syrup is added, turn the speed up to high and continue whipping until the mixture is a thick consistency, and the bowl is cool.

5. Using nonstick spray, spray a 13x9" baking pan. Dust the inside of the pan with sifted confectioners' sugar.

6. Uncovered, transfer the marshmallows to the fridge, overnight, to set.

7. The following day, take the marshmallows out of the pan and dust with more confectioners' sugar.

8. Using a pizza cutter, cut the marshmallows into even squares, and toss with sugar.

9. Store in an airtight resealable container for up to 21 days.

*Servings will depend on the size of marshmallows

Pecan Blondies

Elevate blondies to a whole new level. Top with an Irish cream white chocolate ganache and dust with gold powder for a show-stopping baked treat.

Servings: 16

Total Time: 3hours

Ingredients:

Ganache:

- 8¾ ounces white chocolate (coarsely chopped)
- Pinch of sea salt flakes
- 1 cup double cream
- ½ cup Irish cream liqueur
- 5¼ ounces pecans (coarsely chopped)
- ½ tsp edible gold powder

Pecan Blondie:

- 3 eggs
- 14 ounces soft light brown sugar
- 8¾ ounces unsalted butter (melted and cooled)
- 10½ ounces plain flour
- 1 tbsp vanilla essence
- 1 tsp baking powder
- ½ tsp sea salt flakes
- 3½ ounces 65-70% cocoa solids dark chocolate (coarsely chopped)
- 3½ ounces pecans (chopped)

Directions:

1. Preheat the main oven to 215 degrees F.

2. Place the chocolate on a rimmed baking tray and bake in the preheated oven for 60-90 minutes, until a rich caramel color. You will need to stir the chocolate 10-15 minutes to prevent it from burning or sticking to the tray. It is important to stir and scrape your chocolate off the bottom of the tray every time.

3. Scatter with sea salt and pour onto a fresh baking tray lined with baking paper. Put to one side, to set.

4. Preheat the main oven to 355 degrees F.

5. To prepare the blondies: Grease and line a deep 8" square cake tin.

6. Add the eggs and sugar to a bowl, and using electric beaters, whisk until fluffy and thick for 3 minutes.

7. Mix in the melted butter, and add the remaining ingredients (flour, vanilla essence, baking powder, sea salt flakes, dark chocolate, and pecans) stirring until just incorporated.

8. Spoon the batter into the prepared baking tin and spread the mixture out into an even layer.

9. Bake in the oven until the top begins to slightly brown and is just set, for 35-40 minutes.

10. Remove from the oven and set aside to cool.

11. For the ganache: Chop the caramelized white chocolate and add to a mixing bowl.

12. Add the cream and Irish cream to a pan and bring to a gentle simmer.

13. Next, pour the cream mixture over the white chocolate and set to one side for 60 seconds before stirring to create a smooth and silky ganache. You may need to use a hand blender to do this.

14. Pour the mixture over the blondie and evenly spread.

15. Before the ganache sets, add the pecans along with the edible gold powder in a bowl and evenly toss to coat the pecans.

16. In an even layer, sprinkle the golden pecans over the chocolate ganache.

17. Then, chill in your fridge until the ganache sets, and the blondie is entirely cooled.

18. Cut into even-sized squares and store in an airtight container for up to 4 days.

Posh Popcorn

This favorite movie night sweet snack is all about the topping, and this popcorn with its boozy twist is the ideal naughty nibble for adults.

Servings: 8-10

Total Time: 35mins

Ingredients:

- 4½ ounces unpopped popcorn
- Nonstick cooking spray
- 3½ ounces caster sugar
- 1¾ ounces liquid glucose
- 3½ ounces butter
- ½ cup Irish cream
- 2 tsp baking soda

Directions:

1. Begin by popping the corn. Add the popcorn to a glass bowl and spray the corn with nonstick cooking spray. Cover with a lid and microwave for 2 minutes, or until the corn has slowed down popping.

2. In a single layer, evenly spread the popcorn out on a parchment paper-lined baking tray.

3. For the coating: In a saucepan, gently heat the caster sugar along with the butter, liquid glucose, and stir until the butter is entirely melted and combined.

4. Next, as soon as the sugar is dissolved, increase the temperature and heat for a couple of minutes. Do not stir during this step.

5. Add the Irish cream and stir to combine fully. It may take a short time for the caramel and Irish cream to become smooth. Keep on the heat for a couple of minutes.

6. Remove from the heat, add the baking soda, and stir well.

7. Tip the mixture over the popcorn and with a spoon, mix to evenly coat for 2-3 minutes.

8. Preheat the main oven to 215 degrees F.

9. Bake the coated popcorn in the oven for 20 minutes, until the caramel begins to crisp.

10. Set aside to cool before serving.

Rocky Road Fudge

If rocky road is your favorite ice cream flavor, then there is no doubt about it, this is the sweet treat for you!

Servings: 12

Total Time: 3hours 20mins

Ingredients:

- Butter (to grease)
- 7 ounces dark chocolate (chopped)
- 3 tbsp + 1 tsp Irish cream liqueur
- 4 tsp unsalted butter
- ⅓ cup sweetened condensed milk
- 3 ounces shortbread cookies (crushed)
- 5 tbsp unsalted pistachio nuts (chopped)
- 7 ounces mini marshmallows
- 5¼ ounces white chocolate (chopped)

Directions:

1. Grease a 3x8" baking tin with butter, then line with parchment; make sure to leave some overhand.

2. Melt together the dark chocolate, Irish cream liqueur, butter, and condensed milk using a double boiler. Take off the heat and stir until silky.

3. Fold in the cookies, pistachio nuts, marshmallows, and ⅔ of the chopped white chocolate.

4. Transfer the mixture to the baking tin and chill for 2-3 hours.

5. Melt the remaining white chocolate using a double boiler. Drizzle over the mixture in the baking tin. Allow to sit for a few minutes before slicing into squares.

6. Keep chilled until ready to serve.

Triple Irish Popsicles

With three Irish favorites: stout beer, cream liqueur, and whiskey, these delicious booze-infused popsicles are most definitely for adults only!

Servings: 10

Total Time: 8hours 15mins

Ingredients:

- 2 cups heavy whipping cream
- ¼ cup Irish stout beer
- ¼ cup Irish cream liqueur
- 1 ounce Irish whiskey
- ½ cup chocolate syrup

Directions:

1. Pour half of the whipping cream into a blender and blitz for 20-30 seconds until thick.

2. Add the beer, cream liqueur, whiskey, and chocolate syrup along with the remaining cream. Blitz for another 20-30 seconds until thickened.

3. Pour the mixture equally into your choice of popsicle mold*.

4. Gently stir the liquid in each mold to remove any air pockets. Freeze for half an hour before inserting popsicle sticks. Return to the freezer and freeze overnight.

5. The popsicles will be soft, so be gentle when removing them from the mold.

*The mixture is enough to make approximately 10 popsicles when using an average-sized mold.

White Chocolate and Irish Cream Truffles

White chocolate and Irish cream liqueur come together to create a velvety-smooth truffle. Indulgent and most definitely addictive!

Servings: 40

Total Time: 8hours 30mins

Ingredients:

- 14 ounces white chocolate
- ½ cup heavy whipping cream
- 2 tbsp Irish cream liqueur
- Confectioner's sugar (to coat)

Directions:

1. Melt the white chocolate using a double boiler and transfer it to a mixing bowl.

2. Add the cream to a saucepan over moderately high heat and bring to a boil. Pour over the melted white chocolate. Add the Irish cream liqueur to the mixing bowl and combine using a handheld blender stick. Allow the mixture to cool completely before transferring to the refrigerator and chilling overnight.

3. Taking 1 tsp of the mixture at a time, roll into balls.

4. Roll each ball in confectioner's sugar to coat and place in a small cupcake liner.

5. Keep chilled until ready to serve.

Drinks

Buttered Toffee Tipple

This tempting tipple tastes just like candy, so next time you are craving for a sweet snack, don't reach for the cookie jar – instead, get shaking!

Servings: 1

Total Time: 4mins

Ingredients:

- Ice cubes
- 1 ounce coffee liqueur
- 1 ounce Irish cream liqueur
- 1 ounce almond liqueur
- 3 ounces half half

Directions:

1. First, fill a highball glass half full with ice cubes.

2. Add the coffee, Irish cream, and almond liqueurs to the glass and stir.

3. Stir in the half half and serve.

Caramel Irish Coffee

Irish coffee just got even more delicious, thanks to the addition of butterscotch schnapps and silky caramel syrup.

Servings: 2

Total Time: 5mins

Ingredients:

- 2 ounces Irish whiskey
- 2 ounces butterscotch schnapps
- 2 ounces Irish cream liqueur
- 5 ounces freshly-brewed coffee
- Whipped cream
- Caramel syrup

Directions:

1. Into two warm mugs, pour 1 ounce whiskey, 1 ounce butterscotch schnapps, and 1 ounce Irish cream liqueur.

2. Divide the coffee between two mugs.

3. Top each portion with a dollop of whip cream and a generous drizzle of caramel syrup.

4. Serve straight away!

Chocolatini

Chocolate lovers everywhere will go crazy for this creamy, dreamy Irish-inspired cocktail.

Servings: 1

Total Time: 3mins

Ingredients:

- ⅓ cup Irish cream liqueur
- 1¾ tbsp vanilla vodka
- ¼ ounce chocolate sauce
- Ice cubes
- Chocolate flakes (to garnish)

Directions:

1. Add the Irish cream to a cocktail shaker. Add the vodka, followed by the chocolate sauce.

2. Add some ice cubes to the cocktail shaker and shake it all about until the mixture is smooth and silky.

3. Strain the cocktail into a glass and garnish with flakes of chocolate.

4. Serve and enjoy.

Festive Eggnog

This creamy eggnog is the ultimate feel-good celebratory boozy drink, and here it features a decadent Irish cream twist.

Servings: 4

Total Time: 4mins

Ingredients:

- 4 eggs (beaten)
- 4 tbsp caster sugar
- ½ cup Irish cream liqueur
- 1¼ cups milk
- 1 vanilla pod (split)
- 4 cinnamon sticks (to garnish)
- Cocoa powder (to garnish)

Directions:

1. In a bowl, beat the eggs along with the caster sugar until the sugar is entirely dissolved and the liquid is smooth.

2. Add the Irish cream followed by the milk and split vanilla pod and vigorously whisk to create a silky smooth liquid.

3. Strain the mixture and remove and discard the pod.

4. Pour the eggnog into 4 glasses and garnish with a stick of cinnamon and a dusting of cocoa powder.

Gaelic White Russian

Switch regular cream for Irish cream liqueur and give this Eastern European cocktail a little Gaelic flair.

Servings: 1

Total Time: 3mins

Ingredients:

- Ice cubes
- 3½ tbsp Irish cream liqueur
- 1¾ tbsp premium vodka
- 1 tbsp coffee liqueur
- 5 tbsp whole milk
- Cherry (to garnish)

Directions:

1. Add ice cubes to a tumbler glass.

2. Next, add the Irish cream liqueur followed by the vodka and coffee liqueur, and milk.

3. Mix until silky smooth and chilled.

4. Garnish with a cherry and enjoy.

Irish Coffee Milkshake

A boozy milkshake will definitely bring all the boys to the yard!

Servings: 2

Total Time: 20mins

Ingredients:

Coffee Chocolate Syrup:

- 1 tbsp cocoa powder
- ½ cup sugar
- ½ cup strong coffee
- ½ cup water
- Pinch of salt

Milkshake:

- ½ cup milk
- ½ cup espresso
- 2 cups vanilla ice cream
- ¼ cup Irish cream liqueur
- Whipped cream (to garnish)

Directions:

1. For the syrup: In a pan, combine the water with the strong coffee, cocoa powder, sugar, and salt. Bring to simmer. Them, continue to cook until the syrup reduces and thickens.

2. Remove the pan from the heat and allow the syrup to cool.

3. For the shake: In a food blender, combine the vanilla ice cream with the espresso, Irish cream liqueur, and milk. Process to a smooth consistency.

4. Next, swirl the coffee chocolate syrup into chilled milk glasses.

5. Then, pour in the shake and garnish with a drizzle more of syrup and whipped cream.

6. Enjoy.

Irish Flag Shooter

Celebrate St Patrick's Day with this patriotic green, white, and orange shot.

Servings: 1

Total Time: 2mins

Ingredients:

- ½ ounce Crème de Menthe
- ½ ounce Irish cream liqueur
- ½ ounce orange liqueur

Directions:

1. In a shot glass, layer the liqueurs in recipe order (crème de menthe, Irish cream, and orange liqueur).

2. Sláinte!

Orange Dreamsicle

Irish cream liqueur and zesty orange juice are the perfect pairings, and here they come together to create a marriage made in cocktail heaven.

Servings: 1

Total Time: 4mins

Ingredients:

- 1½ ounces Irish cream
- 3½ ounces fresh orange juice
- Slice of orange (to garnish)

Directions:

1. In an old-fashioned glass, combine the Irish cream with the fresh orange juice.

2. Lastly, garnish with a slice of orange. Enjoy.

Author's Afterthoughts

I would like to express my deepest thanks to you, the reader, for making this investment in one my books. I cherish the thought of bringing the love of cooking into your home.

With so much choice out there, I am grateful you decided to Purch this book and read it from beginning to end.

Please let me know by submitting an Amazon review if you enjoyed this book and found it contained valuable information to help you in your culinary endeavors. Please take a few minutes to express your opinion freely and honestly. This will help others make an informed decision on purchasing and provide me with valuable feedback.

Thank you for taking the time to review!

Christina Tosch

About the Author

Christina Tosch is a successful chef and renowned cookbook author from Long Grove, Illinois. She majored in Liberal Arts at Trinity International University and decided to pursue her passion of cooking when she applied to the world renowned Le Cordon Bleu culinary school in Paris, France. The school was lucky to recognize the immense talent of this chef and she excelled in her courses, particularly Haute Cuisine. This skill was recognized and rewarded by several highly regarded Chicago restaurants, where she was offered the prestigious position of head chef.

Christina and her family live in a spacious home in the Chicago area and she loves to grow her own vegetables and herbs in the garden she lovingly cultivates on her sprawling estate. Her and her husband have two beautiful children, 3 cats, 2 dogs and a parakeet they call Jasper. When Christina is not hard at work creating beautiful meals for Chicago's elite, she is hard at work writing engaging e-books of which she has sold over 1500.

Make sure to keep an eye out for her latest books that offer helpful tips, clear instructions and witty anecdotes that will bring a smile to your face as you read!

Printed in Great Britain
by Amazon

51206417R00068